Blessed Carlo Acutis
1991 - 2006

PRAY FOR US

There is a Marian "thread" that weaves through Blessed Carlo's journey to holiness: from his baptism at a church dedicated to the Virgin Mary in London - Our Lady of Dolours - to consecrating himself to Mary, as a young child, before the miraculous image of Our Lady of the Rosary in Pompei, to promising to recite the Rosary every day at the Grotto of Our Lady of Lourdes. Carlo knew that praying the Rosary was one of the steps to being a saint, indeed, *"the shortest ladder to Heaven"*. Hence, he could speak of the Holy Rosary as *"the most gracious appointment of the day"*. Let us do like Carlo - and you and I can also become saints!

Monsignor. Anthony Figueiredo
Author of "Blessed Carlo Acutis. 5 Steps to Being a Saint"

Pray the Rosary

with

Blessed
Carlo Acutis

"The shortest
ladder
to Heaven"

The Eucharist is my highway to heaven

Blessed Carlo Acutis

On October 8, 2006, Carlo Acutis, a vibrant 15-year-old teenager from Milan, Italy, was rushed to hospital. That day he was diagnosed with one of the worst and most aggressive forms of acute leukaemia. Three days later, on October 11, he fell into a coma and tragically died.

Carlo was buried in Piedmont, a region in the north of Italy and news of the death of this extraordinary young man travelled far and wide. But why?

Carlo was an ordinary teenage boy, a whizz kid in computer programming, website development and videography. He loved playing his saxophone and playing with his pets.
But there was something quite different about this young man. He went to Holy Mass daily for the Eucharist, which he called his *"highway to heaven"* since the age of 7.

He loved adoration, spending hours in front of the Blessed Sacrament, and he couldn't walk by a church without wanting to enter. He was a special kid who was very popular at school. Generous with his time for others, he was always there to help those who needed computing assistance and befriended anyone who needed help.

On the day of his funeral, the church was packed with people from all over Milan, his parents and classmates didn't even know; the homeless, immigrants, beggars, people from all walks of life, rich and poor, whom Carlo befriended on his walk to and from school. Almost immediately after the funeral, countless reports of miracles, graces, favours and spiritual conversions came flooding in. This was the start of the journey to sainthood for this young man.

Blessed Carlo Acutis

Carlo constantly used the treasures of the Catholic church;
the Eucharist, confession and the Rosary.
Through the simplicity of the life of this teenage boy,
Carlo shows us how we, too, can strive to be a saint.

Carlo has no writings like the great doctors of the church, like
St. Therese of Lisieux or St Augustine.
All we have are what he said, his little quotes and phrases,
during his short life. And it is in these little quotes that we see a
glimpse into the incredible evangelical witness of faith Carlo was
to all those around him. We see his profound understanding
and love of the Eucharist, of confession and Mary, our Blessed
Mother.

Carlo was devoted to Our Lady. *"The Virgin Mary is the only
woman in my life,"* he used to say, and he called the Rosary,
which he prayed daily, the *"shortest ladder to heaven"* and the
"most powerful weapon after the Eucharist to fight the devil".

Just as Carlo recognised the power of the intercession of Our
Lady, you are invited to embark on an encounter with Mary, to
bring you closer to Jesus.

Use this booklet as a way to bring the Rosary into your daily
prayer life. And as you meditate on the life of Jesus through the
decades, reflect too on the simplicity of quotes from
Blessed Carlo Acutis that we may imitate his life to bring us
closer to the hearts of Jesus and Mary.

Blessed Carlo Acutis

Carlo loved Assisi, the birthplace of Saint Francis and where he said he felt the *"happiest of all"*. He wanted to be buried in Assisi, and so in January 2007, Carlo's body was transferred to the municipal Assisi cemetery.

Six years after his death, on 12 October 2012, the cause for Carlo's Beatification and Canonisation was officially opened, and he became "Servant of God", and on 5 July 2018, Pope Francis declared Carlo Venerable.

On 12 October 2013, in Brazil, a gravely ill young boy with a congenital disease of the pancreas, causing constant vomiting and rejection of any food, touched a reliquary holding Carlo's relic. "*I wish I could stop vomiting so much",* the young boy exclaimed. That evening he asked for steak, rice and beans! And it was this healing miracle, formally recognised by the Church and attributed to the intercession of Venerable Carlo Acutis, which led to his Beatification.

In January 2019, Carlo's body was exhumed from the Assisi cemetery. The body was found to be still intact, and in April 2019, Carlo's body was moved to the Shrine of the Renunciation in Assisi and is placed behind a glass tomb wearing his favourite outfit, jeans and Nike sneakers.

On 10 October 2020, Carlo was beatified in the Basilica of Saint Francis of Assisi.

Blessed Carlo Acutis, Pray for us!

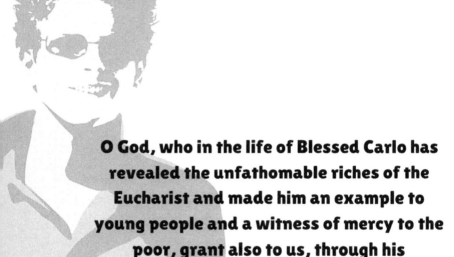

O God, who in the life of Blessed Carlo has revealed the unfathomable riches of the Eucharist and made him an example to young people and a witness of mercy to the poor, grant also to us, through his intercession, to live always united to you and to recognise you in our brothers whom we meet along our way.

Feast Day 12 October

Joyful mysteries

Sorrowful mysteries

Glorious mysteries

Mysteries of light

Daily prayers

"I never fail to keep the most gracious appointment of the day: recitation of the Holy Rosary"

The prayers of the Rosary

In the name of the Father, and of the Son and the Holy Spirit

The Apostles Creed

I believe in God the Father almighty,
Creator of heaven and earth.
And in Jesus Christ, His only Son,
our Lord, Who was conceived by the Holy Spirit,
born of the Virgin Mary,
suffered under Pontius Pilate,
was crucified, died, and was buried.
He descended into hell; the third day
He rose again from the dead;
He ascended into heaven, and sits at
the right hand of God the Father
almighty, from thence He shall come
to judge the living and the dead.
I believe in the Holy Spirit,
the holy Catholic Church,
the communion of saints,
the forgiveness of sins,
the resurrection of the body
and life everlasting.
Amen.

The prayers of the Rosary

Our Father

Our Father who art in heaven,
hallowed be thy name.
Thy kingdom come.
Thy will be done
on earth, as it is in heaven.
Give us this day
our daily bread,
and forgive us our trespasses,
as we forgive those who trespass against us,
and lead us not into temptation,
but deliver us from evil. Amen.

Hail Mary

Hail, Mary, full of grace,
the Lord is with thee.
Blessed art thou amongst women
and blessed is the fruit of thy womb,
Jesus.
Holy Mary, Mother of God,
pray for us sinners,
now and at the hour of our death.
Amen.

Glory be to the Father

Glory be to the Father
and to the Son
and to the Holy Spirit,
as it was in the beginning
is now, and ever shall be
world without end. Amen.

The prayers of the Rosary

The Fatima Decade Prayer
O my Jesus, forgive us our sins;
save us from the fires of hell.
Lead all souls to Heaven,
especially those who are most in need
of your mercy.

Hail, Holy Queen
Hail, Holy Queen, Mother of Mercy, Hail our life, our
sweetness and our hope.
To Thee do we cry,
poor banished children of Eve.
To Thee do we send up our sighs, mourning and
weeping in this vale of tears. T
urn then, Most gracious Advocate,
Thine eyes of mercy towards us,
and after this our exile show unto us the blessed Fruit
of Thy womb, Jesus.
O Clement, O Loving, O Sweet Virgin Mary.

V. Pray for us, O Holy Mother of God.
R. *That we may be made worthy of the promises of Christ.*

Let Us Pray (The Rosary Prayer)
Let us Pray. O God, whose only begotten Son, by His life,
death, and resurrection, has purchased for us the rewards
of eternal salvation. Grant, we beseech Thee, that while
meditating on these mysteries of the most holy Rosary of
the Blessed Virgin Mary, that we may imitate what they
contain and obtain what they promise, through Christ our
Lord. Amen. Most Sacred Heart of Jesus, have mercy on us.
Immaculate Heart of Mary, pray for us.

Joyful mysteries

"I never fail to keep the most gracious appointment of the day: recitation of the Holy Rosary"

The Annunciation

"You too can be a saint"

"Do not be afraid, Mary, for you have found favour with God. Behold, you will conceive in your womb and bear a son, and you shall name him Jesus"

Luke 1: 30-31

The Visitation
"Not I, but God"

When Elizabeth heard the greeting of Mary, the child leaped
in her womb, and Elizabeth was filled with the Holy Spirit
and she exclaimed with a loud cry, "Blessed are you among
women, and blessed is the fruit of your womb"

Luke 1: 41-42

The Nativity

"Everyone is born as an original, but many people end up dying as photocopies"

Mary gave birth to her first born son and wrapped him in swaddling clothes, and laid him in a manger

Luke 2:7

The Presentation of Our Lord in the Temple

"Heaven has been waiting for us for ever"

When the time came for their purification according to the law of Moses, they brought him up to Jerusalem to present him to the Lord

Luke 2: 22

The Finding of Our Lord in the Temple

"From whatever point of view you look, life is always fantastic"

After three days they found him in the temple, sitting among the teachers, listening to them and asking them questions; and all who heard him were amazed at his understanding and his answers

Luke 2: 46-47

Sorrowful mysteries

"I never fail to keep the most gracious appointment of the day: recitation of the Holy Rosary"

Agony in the Garden

"There are others suffering much more than me"

"Watch and pray that you may not enter into temptation, the sprit indeed is willing, but the flesh is weak"

Matthew 26:41

The Sourging at the Pillar

"Saddness is looking at ourselves, happiness is looking towards God"

Pilate said "I am innocent of this righteous man's blood..." and having scourged Jesus delivered him to be crucified

Matthew 27:24; 26

The Crowning with Thorns

"I am happy to die because I have lived my life without wasting a minute on those things which do not please God"

And they stripped him and put a scarlet robe upon him, and plaiting a crown of thorns they put it on his head, and put a reed in his right hand. And kneeling before him they mocked him, saying, "Hail, King of the Jews!"

Matthew 27:28-29

The Carrying of the Cross

"Golgotha is for everyone. No one escapes the cross"

And when they came to a place called Golgotha (which means the place of a skull), they offered him wine to drink, mingled with gall; but when he tasted it, he would not drink it

Matthew 27: 33

The Crucifixion

"Death is the start of new life"

"It is finished";
and he bowed his head and gave up his spirit

John 19: 30

Glorious mysteries

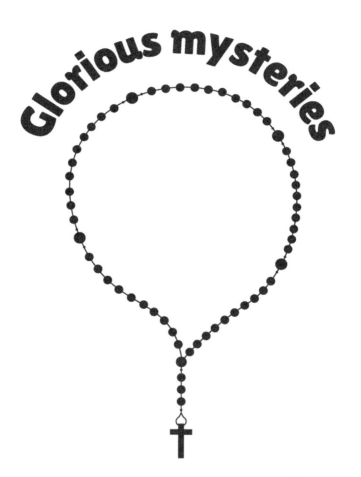

"I never fail to keep the most gracious appointment of the day: recitation of the Holy Rosary"

The Resurrection

"Mama, I will give you signs that I am with God"

*""Why do you seek the living among the dead?
He is not here, but has risen"*

Luke 24:4

The Ascension

"You go straight to Heaven if you participate in the Mass every day"

"Men of Galilee, why do you stand looking into heaven? This Jesus, who was taken up from you into heaven, will come in the same way as you saw him go into heaven"

Acts 1:10-11

Descent of the
Holy Spirit

"Act like me and you will see the results"

And they were all filled with the Holy Spirit and began to speak in other tongues, as the Spirit gave them utterance

Acts 2:3

The Assumption

"The heart of Jesus and the heart of Mary are linked indissolubly, and when we receive

Communion, we are in direct contact with our lady and the saints in paradise."

Blessed art thou of the most high God above all the women upon the earth

Judith 13:1

The Coronation of Mary

"The virgin mother is the only woman in my life"

And a great sign appeared in heaven, a woman clothed with the sun, with the moon under her feet, and on her head a crown of twelve stars

Revelations 12: 1

Luminous mysteries

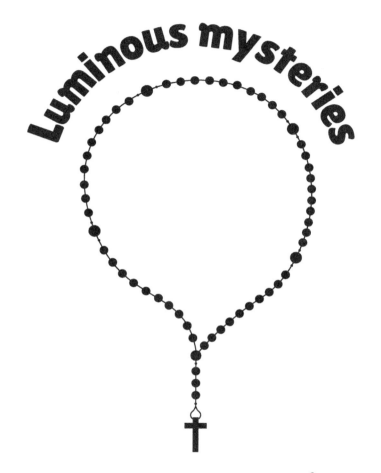

"I never fail to keep the most gracious appointment of the day: recitation of the Holy Rosary"

The Baptism of Christ in the Jordan

"Jesus, come right in. Make youself at home."

"'This is my beloved Son, with whom I am well pleased"

Matthew 3:17

The Wedding Feast at Cana

"The tears and sorrows of the Virgin Mary, who as his mother, can intercede for us more than anyone else can"

When the wine failed, the mother of Jesus said to him, "They have no wine." And Jesus said to her, "O woman, what have you to do with me? My hour has not yet come." His mother said to the servants, "Do whatever he tells you"

John 2:3-6

Proclamation of the Kingdom

"A life will be really beautiful if we come to love God above all things and our neighbour as ourselves"

Jesus began to preach, saying, "Repent, for the kingdom of heaven is at hand"

Matthew 4:17

The Transfiguration

"Each person reflects the light of God"

And a voice came out of the cloud, saying,
"This is my Son, my Chosen; listen to him!"

Luke 9:34

The Institution of the Eucharist

"The Eucharist is my highway to heaven"

Jesus took bread, and blessed, and broke it, and gave it to the disciples and said, "Take, eat; this is my body." And he took a cup, and when he had given thanks he gave it to them, saying, "Drink of it, all of you; for this is my blood of the covenant, which is poured out for many for the forgiveness of sins

Matthew 26:26-28

Daily prayers

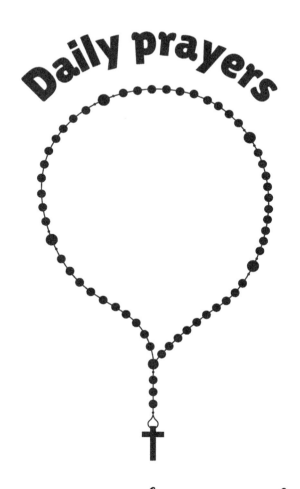

"Prayer is the soul of hope"

Pope Francis

Catholic Prayers

Angel of God

Angel of God,
my guardian dear,
to whom God's love commits me here,
ever this day/night be at my side,
to light and guard, to rule and guide.
Amen.

Prayer to Saint Joseph

Hail, Guardian of the Redeemer,
Spouse of the Blessed Virgin Mary.
To you God entrusted his only Son;
in you Mary placed her trust;
with you Christ became man.
Blessed Joseph, to us too,
show yourself a father
and guide us in the path of life.
Obtain for us grace, mercy and courage,
and defend us from every evil. Amen.

Prayer to Saint Michael Archangel

Saint Michael Archangel, defend us in battle,
be our protection against the wickedness and
snares of the devil; may God rebuke him, we
humbly pray; and do thou,
O Prince of the heavenly host, by the power of God,
cast into hell Satan and all the evil spirits who prowl
through the world
seeking the ruin of souls. Amen.

Catholic Prayers

Prayer to the Holy Family

Jesus, Mary and Joseph,
in you we contemplate
the splendour of true love;
to you we turn with trust.
Holy Family of Nazareth,
grant that our families too
may be places of communion and prayer,
authentic schools of the Gospel
and small domestic churches.
Holy Family of Nazareth,
may families never again experience v
iolence, rejection and division;
may all who have been hurt or scandalized
find ready comfort and healing.
Holy Family of Nazareth,
make us once more mindful
of the sacredness and inviolability of the family,
and its beauty in God's plan.
Jesus, Mary and Joseph,
Graciously hear our prayer.
Amen.

"The Eucharist is truly the heart of Jesus"

"If we go out in the sun, we get a suntan. But when we get in front of Jesus in the Eucharist, we become saints"

"Always to be united with Jesus, this is my programme of life"

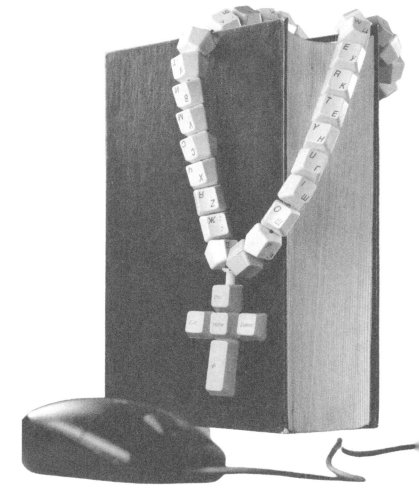

Official prayer for the canonisation of Blessed Carlo Acutis

Oh, Father,
who has given us the ardent testimony,
of the young Blessed Carlo Acutis,
who made the Eucharist the core of his life
and the strength of his daily commitments
so that everybody may love You above all else,
let him soon be counted
among the Saints in Your Church.

Confirm my faith,
nurture my hope,
strengthen my charity,
in the image of young Carlo
who, growing in these virtues,
now lives with You.

Grant me the grace that I need …

I trust in You, Father,
and your Beloved Son Jesus,
in the Virgin Mary, our Dearest Mother,
and in the intervention of
Your Blessed Carlo Acutis.

Our Father.....
Hail Mary.....
Glory Be.....

Acknowledgements:
All images used in the production of this booklet are
used with kind permission from the official Carlo Acutis website

info@carloacutis.com - www.carloacutis.com
To ask for relics: reliquie@carloacutis.com
To ask for prayers: preghiere@carloacutis.com